PERIOD.

PERIOD.

JoAnn Gardner-Loulan
Bonnie Lopez
Marcia Quackenbush

Illustrated by Marcia Quackenbush

New Glide Publications, Inc.

Copyright © 1979 by JoAnn Gardner-Loulan,
Bonnie Lopez and Marcia Quackenbush
All Rights Reserved
Illustrations Copyright © 1979 by Marcia Quackenbush

Library of Congress Cataloging in Publication Data

Gardner-Loulan, JoAnn.
  Period.

  Originally published by My Mama's Press,
Burlingame, Calif.
  SUMMARY: Discusses menstruation and other
related mental and physical changes girls
experience, gives suggestions for coping with these
changes, and explains what happens during a pelvic
exam.
  1. Menstruation — Juvenile literature.
[1. Menstruation] I. Lopez, Bonnie, joint author,
II. Quackenbush, Marcia, joint author.
III. Title.
QP263.G37   612.662   79-25897
ISBN 0-912078-67-7 (formerly ISBN 0-9602324-4-3)

Order directly from: New Glide Publications
                     330 Ellis St.
                     San Francisco, CA   94102

                     Please add .75 for postage and
                     handling. California residents please
                     add appropriate sales tax.

Printed in the United States of America

Contents

This book is dedicated to Billie Gardner Loulan, R.N.

We appreciate those women who allowed us to print their experiences on these pages. There were many other friends who helped and supported us throughout the writing of this book. We would especially like to thank:

Joani Blank, Publisher
Sandy Fujita, Author
Jeanne McFarland, R.N.
Katharine and Larry Moore of Ramparts Press
Nici Muller, M.D.
New Seed Press
JoAnn Ogden, Printer
Our Health Clinic
Judith Supnik, Printer/Editor

Layout and design by Kathleen Moore
                              Marcia Quackenbush

Introduction

Three of us, Bonnie, JoAnn and Marcia, wrote this book for girls who are growing up. We thought it would be important to have a book explaining some of the changes all girls go through. We talked about all kinds of things as we wrote the book, and we learned from the experiences that we shared with our friends. We've put some of the things they said in this book.

It might be interesting for you to talk to your friends as you're going through the chapters. We all have a lot to learn from each other.

Have a good time reading and looking at the pictures.

So Many Changes

Magazines, billboards, television and movies show girls and women who are tall and slim, have faces with no pimples, never wear glasses and seem to have no big problems at all. Not too many people really are that way, but when we see so many women like that it can make us feel that somehow our body or face or hair is just not right.

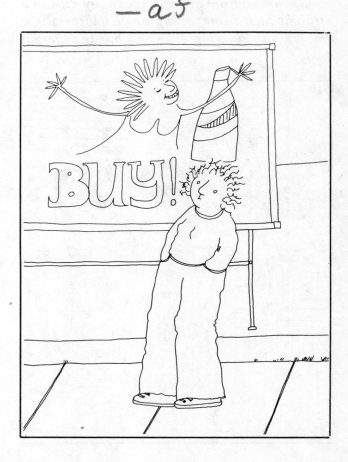

I used to drive myself crazy when I was growing up because I had no waist. Everyone I saw at school or on the street had tiny waists — everyone but me. So I would diet and not let myself eat things that everyone else ate. Know what happened? I lost weight and still had no waist! Then I finally caught on that I had a certain body type and no matter what I ate, I would just go from my rib cage to my hips in a straight line. I am feeling much better about myself just knowing everyone has a different body.

I used to hate the hair on my upper lip. My hair is black, so it's really noticeable. Then I met a girl at school who was just like me and I would watch her when the kids teased her. It really surprised me because it didn't bother her at all! That's when I stopped worrying.

We live in a crazy, mixed-up world because many girls and women think that everyone else has the longest hair or smallest feet, nicest smile or prettiest eyes. But what most people have in common is that we have bodies that can do so many different things, no matter what color, size or shape we are.

We can walk or read or sing or take bubble baths; we can taste wonderful foods or throw balls or listen to birds chirping or dance or run or think or laugh. Sometimes bodies can make us feel soooo gooood! Can you imagine what you'd do without one?

Some of us have bodies that are disabled. This means that some part of the body can't be moved (is paralyzed) or moves uncontrollably (is spastic). Maybe we are blind or deaf or we have a leg or an arm that didn't grow as long as the other. Or a part of our body had to be removed (amputated) because something was wrong with it. Lots of people have these kinds of bodies and it's important that we all learn to appreciate the wonderful things our bodies can do for us. Disabled people can do things that "able-bodied" people can't. "Able-bodied" people can do things disabled people can't. This doesn't mean one person is better than another, it just means that we're different.

One reason we all have different bodies is because of our parents. They have passed some things about their bodies on to us, like the color of our eyes, skin and hair, or how tall we are. You might have your mother's hair color and your father's eyes. But sometimes we think we really can't be happy unless we look like our favorite movie star or girlfriend or aunt. Being comfortable with your own body is important. Learning to love your own specialness is a big part of growing up.

Since your birth, your body has been changing and growing. When you get to be ten or twelve or fourteen, more obvious changes begin to happen. You may begin getting pimples, and the hair under your arms and on your legs may be easier to see. Some people start to sweat (perspire), and perspiration may smell different as you grow older. Your hips get bigger, your breasts begin to grow, and your body actually begins to change shape. The area around your nipple, called the *areola* (ah-REE-oh-la), becomes a little raised and might change color. You might begin growing taller at this age. You will also probably start growing hair on the area below your belly button, close to your legs. This is called *pubic* (PEW-bik) hair.

When I was growing pubic hair, I thought something was wrong with me so I began pulling it out with tweezers. I realized it was normal when I just couldn't pull it out fast enough. But it sure was scary at first!

8

It seems that all of a sudden you are running around with a new body, and it may take some getting used to. You may be the first one in school to show breasts or the last one to gain some weight and start looking older. Maybe your parents or older sisters and brothers will tease and embarrass you. Boys or other girls may make fun of your new bra. You may not believe this, but few of us are comfortable with these changes.

Can you think of three things you really like about your body? Do you like the color or softness of your skin? How about your legs or hands? You really are a special person, and the more you realize that, the better you will feel about yourself.

So Many Parts

Some of the changes your body goes through as you grow older are easy to see, but others go on inside of your body. Even though you don't usually see these changes, they affect your life and the way you feel.

There are a lot of diagrams in this chapter and the next. These diagrams will help explain things, but remember that every woman is different and none of the diagrams will really be exactly like you or anyone else. They can give you an idea of shapes and where things are.

There are quite a few organs inside of us. One way to look at them is by a "cross section" diagram. This is a cross section of an apple. You see the lines and shapes and seeds of the inside of the apple.

The internal organs we will be talking about in this chapter are organs only girls and women have.

The body of a girl is different from that of a woman, but it's hard to say exactly when a girl becomes a woman. From the time we are born, bodies start the kinds of changes this book is all about. In a young girl, internal organs (organs that are inside of us) look something like this:

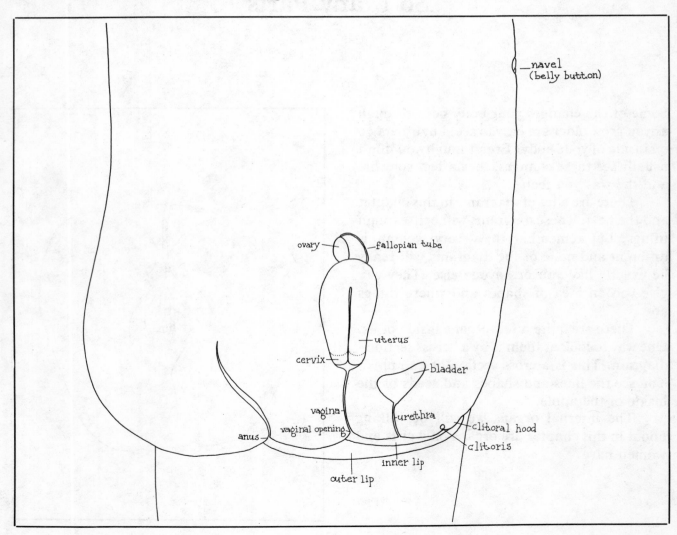

navel (belly button)

ovary — fallopian tube

uterus

cervix

bladder

vagina

urethra

vaginal opening

clitoral hood

anus

clitoris

inner lip

outer lip

This diagram is of an adult woman:

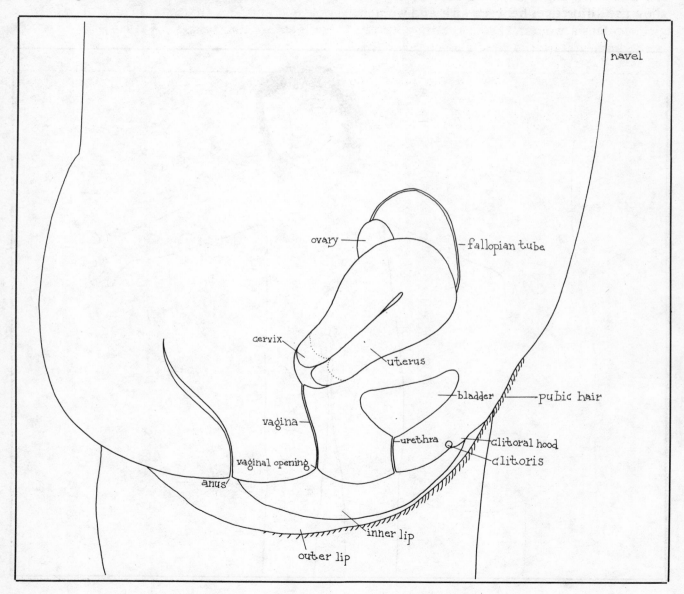

On these two pages are diagrams which also
show the differences between girls and women.

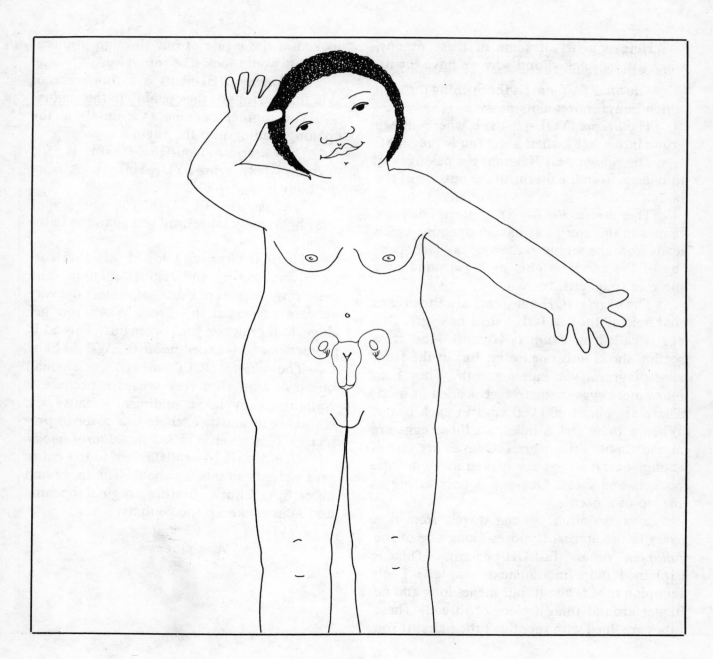

Here is a list of some of these organs, what they are called and why we have them:

The *anus* (AY-nus) is the opening through which bowel movements pass.

The *uterus* (YOU-ter-us) is where an egg grows into a baby when a woman is pregnant.

The *vagina* (vah-JIE-nah) is a passageway that leads from the uterus to the outside of the body.

The *cervix* (SER-vix) protects delicate tissues in the uterus. It has an opening which leads from the uterus to the vagina. The opening of the cervix is only as big around as a piece of spaghetti.

The *ovaries* (OH-vah-reez) are the organs that hold all the *ova* (OH-vah) (the eggs). One egg is called an *ovum* (OH-vum). The cross section shows only one ovary, but in the front view diagram, you can see both. They hold many more eggs than are ever needed or used. There are about 400,000 eggs in each ovary. When a baby girl is born, all those eggs are already in her little ovaries. Ovaries are sort of spongy and the eggs are tucked away in little pockets and folds. One egg is only as big as the tip of a needle.

Every so often, an egg travels from one ovary to the uterus. It moves along one of the *fallopian tubes* (fa-LOH-pee-an). (This is explained more in the next chapter.) Each fallopian tube is about four inches long and no bigger around than a piece of thread. These tubes are lined with very tiny little hairs. If you looked at the inside of one through a microscope, it would look like soft velvet.

The *hymen* (HI-men) is a thin piece of skin that surrounds the opening to the vagina.

The *vaginal opening* (VA-jin-al) is the opening leading into the vagina.

The *urethra* (you-REE-thrah) is the opening where *urine* (YUR-rin) passes from the body.

The *bladder* (BLAD-der) is where your body holds your urine until you go to the bathroom.

The *inner lips* are folds of skin that surround the urethra and vaginal opening. The *outer lips* are pads of skin that protect the very delicate tissues in this area. When you get older, hair grows on your outer lips. This adds protection and is called *pubic* (PEW-bik) hair.

The *clitoris* (CLIT-tor-iss) is a small bump of skin. It's very sensitive because it contains many nerve endings. Because the clitoris is so sensitive, there is a cover to protect it. This cover is called the *clitoral hood*.

Genitals (JEN-a-tulls) refers to the entire area we've been talking about. The inner and outer lips, clitoris, urethra, vaginal opening and anus make up the genitals.

The uterus is an interesting organ. It seems like it should be very large since a baby might have to fit inside of it someday. But it really isn't big at all. It's about the size of your fist. When a woman becomes pregnant, the uterus grows in size with the baby, and after the baby is born, the uterus becomes small again. There are some cut-outs on page 89. One shows the size of the uterus of a woman about twenty-five years old. The other shows the size of a twelve-year-old girl's uterus. If you cut out these pictures and hold them up to your stomach, under your belly button, you might get a better idea of how big your uterus is.

The vagina is another organ which seems like it should be larger because a baby has to travel through the vagina when it's being born. But during birth, the vagina stretches. The sides of the vagina, called the vaginal walls, usually lie close together, touching, like a balloon with no air in it. There isn't a large space at all.

cowrie

scallop

star turrid

In Chapter 1 we talked about the changes that you see and feel as you grow older, like getting taller or having your breasts grow. This chapter described some of the changes that go on inside of you, changes you can't see. Even though our genitals are outside of our bodies, we don't see them very often.

Like most parts of our bodies, genitals change as we get older too, but often we don't notice. We rarely look at our genitals because they are tucked away. When you're young, it looks as if you don't have any inner lips at all. They're very small. When you're older, your inner lips grow larger, but exactly how much they grow is different for all of us.

Just like her smile or the color of her hair, everyone's genitals are a little different. It might help to think of flowers or sea shells — no two flowers will ever be quite the same even if they're the same kind of flower.

arabis

iris

marguerite

hyacinth

tiger lily

phlox

Menstruation

Part of growing up for a girl is beginning to menstruate. What exactly is this mysterious thing called *menstruation* (MEN-stroo-AY-shun)? Let's talk about it.

At a certain time in your life, maybe when you're ten, or fourteen, or eighteen, the *hormones* (HOR-mones) in your body become very active. Hormones are chemicals your body makes. These hormones, in their own special way, begin telling your body to be alert, pay attention, and start doing things it's never done before. There are hundreds and hundreds of these messages. In this chapter, only a few will be mentioned. It would be confusing to try to keep track of all of them.

One of the first things to happen is that an egg works its way out of one of your ovaries. (Remember that this egg will be no larger than the point of a needle.) This tiny egg floating around wants to get from the ovary to the uterus. That seems like a difficult thing to do, especially since the egg doesn't have any wings to fly with or wheels to roll with. But each fallopian tube has these teeny tiny little hairs at the end of it, almost like fingers. They swoosh back and forth like waves in the ocean, trying to help the egg inside the tube. When this happens, the egg travels all the way through the fallopian tube to the uterus.

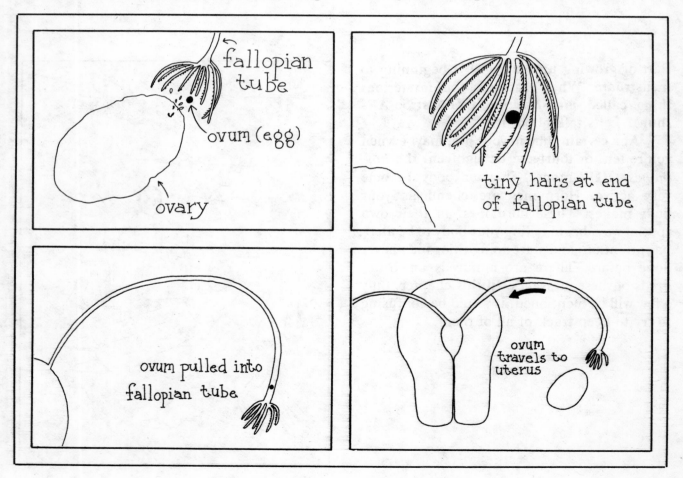

fallopian tube

ovum (egg)

ovary

tiny hairs at end of fallopian tube

ovum pulled into fallopian tube

ovum travels to uterus

At the same time this happens, your uterus begins building up a lining of healthy, fresh tissue and blood. (You can picture what a "lining" is if you think of wallpaper that lies on the walls inside of a house.) By the time the egg reaches the uterus, the lining of the uterus is full and rich and soft. If the egg is going to stay for awhile and become a baby, this lining will make its stay healthy and comfortable. But most of the time, the egg just visits and then passes on through. If the egg isn't staying in the uterus, the uterus doesn't need all that lining, so the lining, made up of blood and tiny pieces of tissue dribbles out. It passes through the small opening in the cervix, down through the vagina and out the vaginal opening. About two weeks later, another egg pops out of one of the ovaries, and the whole cycle starts again. This is what menstruation is all about.

It seems like all this shouldn't take very long because everything is so busy. Actually, though, the whole menstrual cycle takes about a month. The part where your uterus is dribbling blood and lining may last anywhere from two to eight days. It's different for every girl and woman. Once you've started your menstrual cycle, the monthly dribbling of blood will probably keep happening until you're forty or fifty. Then those hormones will send more messages around and your body will stop menstruating.

The next few chapters talk about what menstruation may feel like for you, what you do to catch your menstrual blood, and how to keep an eye on your cycle and stay healthy.

Pads, Pins or Tampons?

Fifty years ago, our grandmothers used pieces of cloth to catch their menstrual blood each month. Today we have so many menstrual products to choose from, it's almost hard to decide which is best to use. It will be easier to choose a product when you know what each is like and how it is used.

SANITARY PADS or SANITARY NAPKINS

Sanitary pads come in different sizes and are made of layers of soft cotton. Some pads are used with a special belt which holds them in place.

A Sanitary belt looks like this:

A pad is fastened to the belt like this:

There are also pads made to be worn without belts or pins. They have a sticky strip that helps them stay in place on your underpants and come off easily when you change pads.

sticky strip

this strip peels off

With pads, one side faces toward your body and one toward your underpants. The side that faces toward your pants usually has a strip, colored string or some design on it, and the side that faces you is usually plain, clean cotton.

cross-section of a sanitary pad:

soft cotton pad

plastic shield to keep blood from staining clothes

It fits under your clothes. If you don't have a belt or don't want to use one, you can also use safety pins and pin a pad onto your underpants.

The first time I wore a pad, it felt so huge and bulky. I was sure everyone could tell I was on my period. I was surprised when I finally looked into a mirror and saw that the pad didn't show at all.

It's true that, for most girls, a pad feels funny at first. But pads fit close to your body and really don't show. If a large pad isn't comfortable, try a smaller size.

TAMPONS

Tampons are another product used to catch menstrual blood. They are made of soft cotton pressed together into this kind of shape:

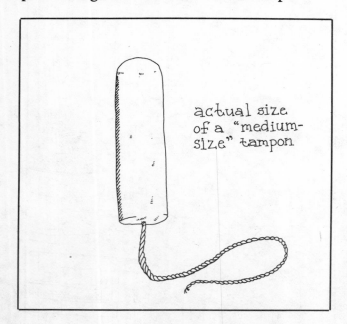

actual size of a "medium-size" tampon

There is a string at the end of the tampon. Tampons fit inside the vagina and the string hangs down through the vaginal opening. When you want to remove a tampon, you pull gently on the string and it comes right out.

Tampons, like pads, come in different sizes. There are junior (small), regular (medium), super (large) and extra large sizes. The first time you try a tampon, a smaller size will probably be easiest.

Some tampons come with an applicator which helps guide the tampon into the vagina. It's thrown away when the tampon's in place. There are cardboard, plastic and stick applicators. Some tampons don't have any applicator. You just use your finger to guide the tampon into your vagina.

cardboard applicator

plastic applicator

stick applicator

no applicator
(you use your finger)

If a tampon is put in the right way, you probably won't be able to feel it at all, but the first time may be confusing.

The first time I used a tampon was terrible. I couldn't understand how to put it into my vagina and the diagram didn't help at all. It looked like I was supposed to stand on my head to put it in. When I finally found my vaginal opening (which took some doing), I only put the tampon in halfway. Guess I was scared if I put it in too far I'd lose it. After twenty minutes, I took it out. Not being in all the way made it very uncomfortable.

There are directions included in every box of tampons. Be sure you read them carefully if you're not sure how to use tampons.

Some girls are afraid they might lose a tampon in their vagina. A tampon really can't get lost inside of you — there's nowhere for it to go. The opening to the uterus is too small for a tampon to get through and the muscles of the vagina keep it from falling out.

Most girls use pads when they first begin their periods. Later you might want to try tampons. The most important thing is for you to be comfortable with your choice. Each girl will find the product that suits her best.

Pads or tampons should be changed at least twice a day, more often when menstrual flow is heavy. When you've finished with a pad or tampon, wrap it up in toilet paper, tissues or newspaper and throw it away. Some people flush tampons down the toilet, but this can clog up some toilets and cause quite a problem.

tampon in place

Once I started my period very late Sunday night and I didn't have any pads or tampons. I got a clean washcloth and folded it so it would comfortably fit me, and used it like a pad. I just rinsed it out in cold water the next morning. It worked very well.

If you are ever caught on your period without pads or tampons, remember what our grandmothers did before the days of menstrual products. Some women even today prefer using a washcloth or similar cloth instead of store bought menstrual pads or tampons.

You may see ads in magazines about vaginal sprays and *douches* (DOOSH-es). A *douche* (DOOSH) is a liquid used to wash the vagina. Vaginal sprays are supposed to help keep you "clean and fresh." But it's been found that, for many women, sprays actually cause infections or rashes. Your vagina cleans itself naturally (like your eyes). The only reason for using a douche is if you have a medical problem and a doctor or health worker suggests you douche.

I Have a Question About That

I had so many questions and scaries about menstruation. No one ever mentioned what was going to happen to me. I saw a film on menstruation in school a year after I began my period. Big help!

Menstruation is a big event in our lives. How we feel about it depends on what our mothers, friends, older sisters, grandmothers or aunts have said. If no one talks about menstruation, it can be very puzzling.

Bodies go through many changes, especially during the teens, and it can help to know what to expect. It's normal to have questions about menstruation. Many girls wonder how old they will be when they begin their periods or how they will know they have started menstruating.

I was upset that I hadn't started menstruating by the time I was sixteen. It seemed like all my girlfriends had already begun having periods. Even my younger sister was menstruating before I was! I was glad when I finally started.

*

When I first menstruated, I bled quite a bit. It scared me because I didn't expect so much blood. Now I know that that's the right amount of blood for my body.

Beginning to menstruate is a unique experience. No one can say exactly what it's going to be like for you, but the more you know about menstruation, the easier it will be.

Menstruation is as normal and natural for girls and women as eating or sleeping. It's a sign that we're changing and it happens at different times for all of us. Some of us begin to menstruate when we're young — maybe nine or ten years old. Some of us don't begin until we're seventeen or eighteen. Because everyone's body is different, menstruation starts at different times. Most girls probably begin at twelve or thirteen. It's not better to begin menstruating at one age or another. It doesn't mean you're more grown up if you start your periods at age ten, or immature if you start at eighteen. Usually your body knows just the perfect time for *you* to begin menstruating.

I wondered how much blood was going to come out of my vagina. Was it going to gush out?

The amount of blood varies from girl to girl, especially during the first couple years of menstruation. A girl may lose as little as one tablespoon of blood or up to six tablespoons in each cycle. The blood doesn't come out all at once. It dribbles and drips out, and a menstrual period may last from two to eight days. Some girls lose more blood on the first day and less on the following days. Some bleed more on the second day. The way each girl menstruates is different.

You might want to try on a pad before you ever start your period. This way you can find out how to put one on and what it's like to wear one. It might be uncomfortable or awkward at first, but planning ahead may clear up confusions now rather than on the first day of your period. Experiment. If you wear a pad that feels very bulky and uncomfortable, try a mini-pad. They're smaller and might be better for you. *You* decide what's best for your body.

What if I start in the middle of my math class?

You also might want to think about what you're going to do if you start your period at school. Here are some suggestions. The first thing you'll want to do is excuse yourself from class. Let your teacher know it is important that you leave the room. If you carry a purse and happen to have a sanitary pad with you, everything should be fine. You have probably practiced beforehand and will already know how to use it. If you don't have a pad with you, your school might have a machine in the girl's bathroom that sells them for ten cents. But what if your school doesn't have a machine, or you don't have a dime, or there is a machine and you have a dime but the machine is empty? Usually the nurse's office will have sanitary pads available for situations like this, so try there next.

If blood has gotten on your underpants, you can probably wait until you get home to wash them out. If you are uncomfortable or blood is showing on your clothes, you should be able to get an excuse from the school nurse to go home and change your clothes.

Once you have started menstruating, you may have a better idea of when your period will begin each month. You can be prepared by carrying a sanitary pad with you, but if your period ever surprises you, the few steps just mentioned should help out.

Your body goes through many changes, especially during the teens when you begin to menstruate. It may take several years for your cycle to balance out and get used to this new process going on inside of you. This means you might miss a period for one month or even for six months. You may have heavy bleeding one month and hardly any at all the next. Later on your body will get into a rhythm and your period may come somewhere between every 26 to 32 days, or approximately once a month. Many books say that women's menstrual cycles come every 28 days, but this is just an average and not the "right" length of time.

A good way to keep track of your period is by marking the days you menstruate on a calendar. You will get an idea of how long you menstruate as well as how many days there are between periods. Menstrual cycles are measured from the day one period begins to the day the next period begins. Once you've started menstruating, if it seems that your cycle isn't regular, you may want to tell somebody (your mother or someone else you feel comfortable with), and get it checked out.

Families and friends can react so differently when a girl begins her period. Sometimes it makes us proud, sometimes embarrassed.

When I began menstruating, my mother told my older brothers, my father, and even the neighbors! Even now I feel sort of embarrassed when I menstruate.

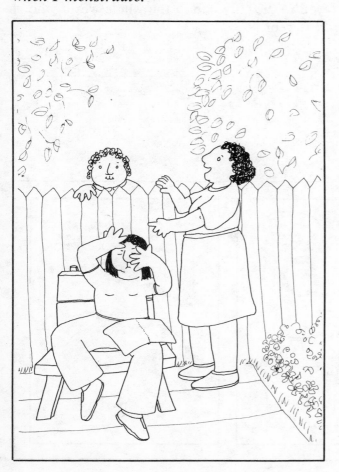

My family had a very special dinner the night I began my period. I felt very proud and good about it and felt a lot of love from my family. I was growing up and they knew it.

It might be interesting for you to find out similar experiences your mother or friends had when they began menstruating. Sometimes it's comforting to talk to someone when something new is happening to you and you feel like you're the only one in the whole world who is different.

DO YOU HAVE TIME TO TALK FOR AWHILE?

SURE!

I'M NOT EVEN SURE WHAT I WANT TO TALK ABOUT.

THAT'S OKAY. WE CAN JUST SIT TOGETHER A BIT.

WELL, IT SEEMS LIKE A LOT OF THINGS IN MY LIFE ARE CHANGING.

WELL, YOU'RE DOING A LOT OF GROWING UP.

42

I enjoy talking about my thoughts and feelings with my friends. I used to be uncomfortable asking my friends certain questions. I got over it because I found people love to talk about themselves. For instance, I would have a strange dream and would think something was wrong with me. The more people I talked to, the more I found out my dreams were not that different from other peoples'.

The same goes for menstruation — the more we talk to people, the more we find out that our experiences, feelings and thoughts can be similar.

Girls and women may get cramps when they menstruate. These cramps can hurt. Some have uncomfortable cramps while others hardly feel any difference at all when they menstruate. Cramps happen when your uterus, which is a muscle, contracts, similar to the way the muscles in your arm tighten up (or contract) when you make a fist.

If you do get cramps, there are several things you can do that might help.

Warmth causes muscles to relax and can help ease cramps. A hot water bottle or heating pad on your stomach may help. (But remember, hot water bottles and heating pads can cause burns if they're used for too long or they're too hot. Check it out with your mother or someone else before using one to make sure you know how to use it correctly.)

A warm bath or drinking something hot like tea or hot chocolate may make you feel better.

Taking a slow walk may help your cramps go away.

Sometimes just rubbing or massaging your stomach can make you feel better. You might try lying on your back with your knees up; move your knees in a small circle. This is a kind of massage too.

Or just try lying in this position. It feels good because your uterus is hanging down, which helps it relax.

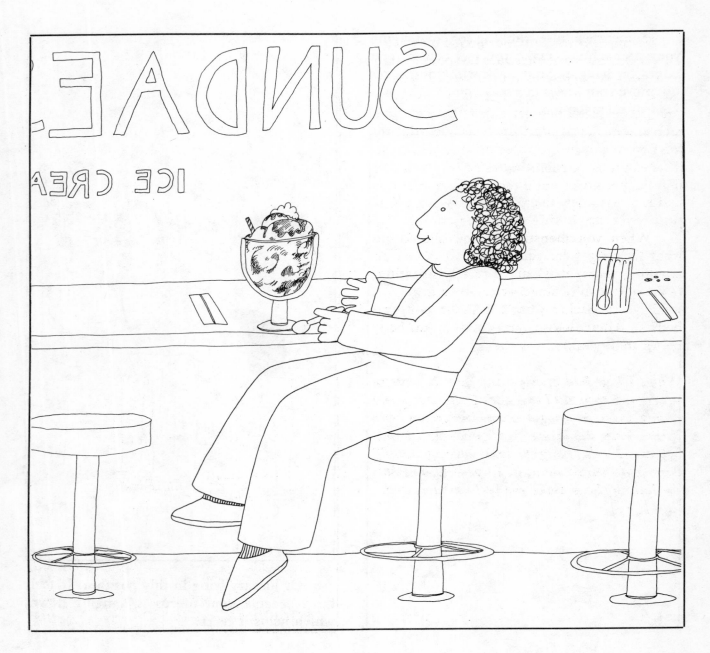

Eating lightly before your period may help. This is because your intestines are packed into your body very close to your uterus. If you've eaten a lot of pizza and hot fudge sundaes, your large intestines get filled up and take more room. Your uterus gets swollen during the first day or two or three of your period, so it takes up more room in the body. By eating lightly, you make more room for your uterus and it is less likely to cramp. Try it out sometime if you are having a lot of cramping.

When you menstruate, you should do what feels right for you. Some of us can do anything we want when we're menstruating. Some of us can't. Since we're all so different, we have to decide what's best for our own bodies. After all, no one knows your body better than *you* do.

When I had bad cramps one day, several of my friends thought I was acting silly because I didn't want to go get some ice cream with them. They made me feel embarrassed only because I was trying to take care of myself. Now that I think about it, I was silly, but only for letting them make me feel embarrassed.

49

For me, having my period was never any big deal. I've never had bad cramps and menstruation doesn't slow me down a bit. I still run and work and do everything I always do. If anything, I guess I have a little more energy during my period than at other times.

*

I used to hate it when I got my period. I thought it got in the way of wanting to do things, like playing basketball. I loved basketball. But now I think of menstruation as my body telling me that everything inside of me is working and that I'm healthy. For me, it's also a time to sit back, relax and be nice to myself. I might make myself a favorite cup of tea and read a book I haven't had time to read. Or I might just sit there and listen to music or daydream. Now, I almost feel like I'm on vacation.

Some people say that it isn't a good idea to go swimming when you are menstruating. Swimming isn't harmful at all. Cool water may make you stop bleeding for awhile and hot water (like a hot bath) may make you bleed a little more heavily. Swimming is okay if you feel like it. You just might be more comfortable wearing a tampon since a pad would get very wet and squishy.

Remember, whatever you do during your period, whether it's playing basketball, reading a book or swimming, really depends on how you feel. There's no right or wrong thing as long as you do what's comfortable for your body.

You may have heard that when you have your period, you have an odor about you that other people can smell. Because heat and air and odors float upwards, we're usually the only ones who can smell our own menstrual blood (if we smell it at all). As long as you wash your genitals with soap and water as usual (or more often if you want to), and change your pad or tampon when necessary, you probably won't have any problems with odor. You may think you're smelly and bothering everyone who comes within two feet of you, but that's because you're so aware of yourself — not because you smell.

During your period, you might get some blood on your underpants. This is very common. If blood stains your pants, use cold water to rinse them out first. It works really well. Then plain old soap and water should get them clean. You could use bleach as a last resort, especially with old stains.

I grew up in a small town, so I knew everyone who worked at the drug store. It was awful for me to have to buy menstrual pads from people I knew, so I always asked my mother to buy them for me.

Sometimes having to go into a store and buy pads or tampons is awkward or embarrassing. It feels like everyone is watching, especially the boys. But, like anything we do again and again, it's not such a big deal after awhile.

Lots of different things have been covered in this chapter. A few of your questions may have been answered, but probably some have been missed. When new questions come up, perhaps you'll talk to somebody you're comfortable with about them.

Why Do I Feel This Way?

As we grow older, we are able to see many changes in our bodies and sometimes our feelings and emotions are changing too. It's natural to have new ideas and feelings at different times in our lives, but because you can't see or touch them, emotions can be confusing.

You may find when you start menstruating that your period affects the way you feel. There are different kinds of feelings girls and women may have and, like so many other things, no two people feel exactly the same. We talked to a lot of women and girls who menstruate and asked them how they feel just before, during or after their periods, and here's what some of them said:

Carol: "When I'm on my period, I feel like I'm just one part of this big exciting world. My menstrual cycle makes me feel like part of the world's cycles — seasons, day and night. It's nice."

Cathy: "I know I'm healthy when my periods are healthy."

Mary: "Sometimes just before my period, I feel sad and
don't know why."

Linda: "I always feel much better about my plants when I'm on my period. I love to sing to them and I think they listen better."

Roxanne: "I write better poems when I'm menstruating."

Lyn: "Usually, I don't mind spending an evening alone, but around the time I menstruate, I feel very lonely if people aren't always around me."

Jennifer: "I always love to take walks in the woods or along the beach, especially when I'm on my period."

Lisa: "Oh, I always feel so ugly when I menstruate. My face usually breaks out and I don't like that at all."

Amy: "I like to take care of myself a lot when I'm having my period. I dress up or buy a new scarf or something."

Ellen: "It seems like sometimes when I'm about to menstruate, I get an urge to reorganize shelves, closets, books. And I have a really good time doing it."

Janet: "If I get cramps, they just make me feel bad and it's hard to have fun that day."

Yvette: "I can get *so* mad sometimes about such little things. Right around the time I menstruate, my temper is very short."

Inez: "I love to spend time with lots of friends when I'm on my period."

Jackie: ". . . and I like to spend lots of time all by myself."

Gloria: "Sometimes I feel like no one understands anything I'm trying to say."

Esther: "If I have time, I always love to bake bread when I'm having my period."

Emily: "I seem to have so little energy the first day of my period."

Delores: "I have more energy than ever about the time I start my period."

Toni: "Seems like I spend a lot of time thinking about serious things, expecially when I'm menstruating."

Laura: "I get hungry for certain foods a day or two before my period. I'll get a real craving for strawberries or scrambled eggs, and I'll raid the refrigerator late at night."

Erica: "I feel so many things, all the time. The best part of being healthy and having my period is that I feel joyous and alive."

There's no one way you *have* to feel or are supposed to feel when you're menstruating. Your period might not make you feel any different at all. Once again, part of what's so wonderful about us is that we are all so different about many things.

What's A Pelvic Exam?

A *pelvic* (PEL-vick) exam is an exam where a doctor or other medical worker checks female organs inside and outside our bodies. A nurse practitioner, gynecologist or regular doctor can do this exam. A *gynecologist* (GUY-nuh-KOL-oh-jist) is a doctor specially trained to take care of these female parts.

Just like regular visits to the dentist, having a pelvic exam is very important. Many physicians think the best time to start having pelvic exams is after your first menstrual period. It is always better for your body to be checked regularly instead of waiting until you're sick. Regular check-ups can prevent sickness, and that's important! It's a good idea to have a pelvic exam every year and, after you're twenty-five, every six months.

I was twenty when I had my first pelvic exam. Oh, was I embarrassed! I went alone, trying to act real grown up and like I knew what was going on, but I was scared. I didn't ask what was going to happen to me and no one told me. This made it hard to go back a year later for my second pelvic exam.

Your first pelvic exam doesn't have to be a scary experience, especially if you know what is going on before it happens. Just reading this chapter may make your first exam easier for you.

When you first get to the doctor's office or clinic, you will be asked to fill out a medical history. For instance, a doctor will want to know what diseases you or your family has had, the length of your menstrual period and the date of your last period. You also might want to tell the nurse or doctor that this will be your first pelvic exam.

If your mother or a girlfriend can go with you, it might make you feel better too. If you'd like to have her go into the exam room with you, call ahead to make sure it's okay with your doctor. The doctor will probably say it's all right, but if not, and if it's important to you, you might want to find another doctor.

You will be asked to come into an exam room. Make sure you go to the bathroom before your exam. This will make it more comfortable for you. Once in the room, a nurse or health worker will ask you to undress and give you a paper dress to put on.

The doctor will first examine your breasts. This is done by gently pressing all around your breasts. She will be checking for any abnormal lumps or breast tissues that might be signs of disease. She can show you how to do a breast exam yourself. You'll want to learn to do this so you can check your breasts regularly between pelvic exams.

Next, your genitals and internal organs will be checked. You will be asked to lie down and put your feet on something called "stirrups." One kind is made so your feet rest on them. Another kind of stirrups is made so the backs of your knees rest on them. Your knees and legs will be spread open so the genital area is easier to see.

For many girls and women, this is the most embarrassing part of the exam. We're just not used to showing a very delicate and private part of ourselves, especially to strangers. This part of the exam might be easier for you if you go to a woman doctor or health worker. But don't forget, whether it's a woman or a man, your doctor has done this hundreds of times. It may be new to you, but she is used to it and is most concerned with your health.

The doctor or health worker will first look at your genitals and see that everything is healthy. Then she will check your internal organs. To do this, she will use a *speculum* (SPECK-you-lum). A speculum is either metal or plastic. It is inserted into your vagina to hold the vaginal walls apart. Then something called a pap smear is taken. A cotton swab is gently touched in your cervical opening to collect some of your cervical tissues. You probably won't feel this at all. These cells are put on a slide and sent to a laboratory. The pap smear is a check to make sure the cells in your cervix are growing normally.

Then the speculum will be removed. The gynecologist will put on a pair of thin rubber gloves. She'll apply a special slippery *gel* (JEL) to her fingers. She will insert one finger into your vagina and with the other hand press down on your stomach. This is the best way to see if your uterus, cervix, ovaries and fallopian tubes feel normal and healthy. If you ask, she will probably let you put your hand on your stomach to feel these organs.

If you have any questions, ask them during your exam. You might even want to make a list to take into the room with you so you don't forget anything. Doctors sometimes don't give much information unless you ask. They've done this many times before and don't realize that you might not know all about it yourself. But remember, it's your body, and you have every right to learn as much as you want about it.

The most important thing to remember about gynecology is to have anything that seems unusual checked out. If you have been feeling anything different around your genitals, like burning or itching or seeing a new kind of discharge (fluid which comes from your vagina), tell your gynecologist. If your breasts hurt or you have any lumps in them, ask your doctor about it. Often when a girl's breasts are growing, there is some tenderness, but a doctor will be able to make sure everything is all right. The more you tell your doctor or health worker, the better and more complete exam she will be able to give you. The better your exam is, the healthier you will be and, after all, that's what we're all aiming for with our pelvic exams.

Conclusion

Well, here we are at the end of this book. We hope you enjoyed looking at it and that it answered many of your questions. There are two important things we'd like you to remember. One is that no two people are ever quite the same.

The other is that we want you to ask questions and get answers to the things about your life that you don't understand. After reading this book, you know more about menstruation than the three of us knew when we were nine or ten years old. We learned a lot about menstruation just writing the book, and when we talked with some of our friends (girls and women both) we found that often they didn't know about some of these things either. We hope that knowing how your body works makes growing up and going through all these changes easier.

Good luck!

girl's
uterus

cut on dotted
lines

woman's
uterus

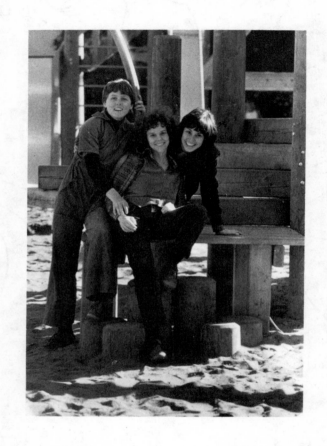

Marcia   Bonnie

          JoAnn

JoAnn Gardner-Loulan is a clinical psychologist dividing her time between private practice and work in a private hospital in San Jose, California. She is associated with the Department of Psychiatry Human Sexuality Program at the University of California, San Francisco Medical School. In her spare time, she enjoys doing close-up photography.

Bonnie Lopez is a health educator who, in the past five years, has taught over 500 adolescents and 9,000 health professionals and medical and nursing students. She is also associated with the Department of Psychiatry Human Sexuality Program at the University of California, San Francisco. Now that her work on this book is finished, she plans to begin a new book and enjoy her pregnancy.

Marcia Quackenbush is a freelance illustrator and graphic designer who has worked and exhibited in the Bay Area for several years. She has a degree in Folklore from San Francisco State University and teaches banjo at the San Francisco School of Folk Music. She loves bluegrass music, art and her dog, Ninotchka.